Wetlands

To the One who created wetlands.

—*Genesis* 1:1

Published by
PEACHTREE PUBLISHERS
1700 Chattahoochee Avenue
Atlanta, Georgia 30318-2112
www.peachtree-online.com

Illustrations created in watercolor on archival quality 100% rag watercolor paper.
Text and titles set in Novarese from Adobe.

Printed in Singapore
10 9 8 7 6 5 4 3 2 1
First Edition

Library of Congress Cataloging-in-Publication Data

Sill, Cathryn P., 1953-
  About habitats : wetlands / written by Cathryn Sill ; illustrated by John Sill.-- 1st ed.
      p. cm.
  ISBN-13: 978-1-56145-432-7 / ISBN 10: 1-56145-432-X
  1. Wetlands--Juvenile literature. I. Sill, John, ill. II. Title.
  QH87.3.S55 2008
  578.768--dc22

                    2007031280

Wetlands

Written by **Cathryn Sill**   Illustrated by **John Sill**

PEACHTREE
ATLANTA

Wetlands can be found on every continent but Antarctica.
They provide homes for thousands of species of plants and animals.

Some Common Types of Wetlands

Bog—a wet, spongy area of standing water where plants such as sphagnum moss grow.

Marsh—an area that is covered with shallow water where plants such as grasses, reeds, and sedges grow.

Swamp—an area that is covered with shallow water where certain shrubs or trees grow.

Vernal Pool—an area that is covered with water for part of the year and is dry the rest of the year.

Wetlands

Wetlands are places that are covered with shallow water.

The water may be fresh or salty.

PLATE 2
PAPYRUS SWAMP (freshwater)
Hippopotamus

SALT MARSH
Northern Raccoon

Some wetlands are under water all the time.

In other wetlands the water drains away or dries up part of the time.

PLATE 4
VERNAL POOL

Eastern Phoebe
Wood Frog

Some wetlands look dry, but the ground is soggy.

Plants in wetlands have special ways of growing. Some have roots in the soil and grow out of the water. Some grow under the water. Others float on top of the water.

Marshes are wetlands where grasses and other plants with soft stems grow.

Swamps are wetlands where trees and shrubs grow.

Only certain types of plants can grow in bogs because the soil is poor.

Many plants that grow in wetlands provide protection for the animals that live there.

PLATE 10
MANGROVE SWAMP

Yellow-crowned Night-Heron
Snook
Striped Mullet
Red Mangrove

Wetlands are good places for some animals to raise their babies.

Wetlands provide food for many animals.

PLATE 12
FRESHWATER MARSH

Tree Swallow
Red-winged Blackbird
Red-necked Grebe
Beaver
Moose

Wetlands provide food for people, too.

Wetlands act like sponges in wet weather. They soak up extra water that might cause floods.

Wetlands along seacoasts help protect the land from bad storms. The plants in wetlands slow the storm waves that wash over the land.

Wetlands help keep Earth's water clean.

Wetlands are very important places that need to be protected.

Afterword

PLATE 1

Wetlands form in areas where water collects. The water may come from precipitation, underground springs, tidal flows, or overflow from rivers and lakes. Wetlands are found on every continent except Antarctica. Greater Flamingos live in tropical wetlands. They get tiny particles of food from water by holding their bills upside down and pumping the water with their tongues. Special grooves on their bills filter the water as it is forced out of their mouths, allowing the food to stay inside.

PLATE 2

Freshwater wetlands are usually found inland. Saltwater wetlands usually form near the coastlines of oceans. The water in most coastal wetlands moves in and out with the tides. Hippopotamuses spend their days resting in freshwater swamps and rivers in Africa. At night they go on land to look for grasses to eat. Northern Raccoons are often found close to fresh or salty wetlands in North and Central America, where they hunt for frogs, fish, mollusks, crustaceans, and insects.

PLATE 3

Permanent wetlands are covered by water all year. They may have deeper water than other types of wetlands. Giant Water Lilies grow in the Amazon River basin of South America. They are the largest water lilies in the world. Their leaves grow over 6 feet wide, and the blooms are up to a foot across.

PLATE 4

Some seasonal wetlands dry up completely in the summer and fill back up in fall, winter, and spring. Fish that eat amphibian eggs and larvae are not able to live in temporary pools, so many types of frogs and toads choose to lay their eggs in vernal (springtime) pools. Wood Frogs live in seasonal and permanent wetlands farther north than any other North American amphibian. They become active in late winter or early spring and may start singing before all the ice has melted from the pools.

PLATE 5

Wet meadows do not have water standing in them most of the year, but the ground stays soggy year-round. Plants that grow in wet meadows are a good source of food for wildlife. While blooming, the meadow flowers provide nectar for butterflies, and after the flowers have died, they provide seeds for birds. Many wet meadows are destroyed when people dig ditches through them or drain them.

PLATE 6

Wetland plants that grow out of the water are called emergents. The roots of emergent plants like Pickerelweed are in the wet soil under the water. Plants that grow completely underwater are called submergents. The roots of submergents like Fanwort can grow in the soil or in the water. The roots of free-floating plants like Water Lettuce hang down under the surface of the water.

PLATE 7

Most freshwater marshes are covered with shallow water all year. They are often found along the edges of rivers, lakes, and ponds. Cattails are common marsh plants all over the world. Marsh Wrens weave their nests from cattail leaves and line them with the fluffy seeds that come from old blooms. The whole plant is edible and was an important source of food for Native Americans and early settlers.

PLATE 8

In the United States, wetlands with woody plants are called swamps. These areas are often identified by the types of plants growing there. Bushes and shorter trees grow in shrub swamps. Tall trees grow in forested swamps. Bald Cypress trees are common in freshwater swamps in the southeastern United States. These trees have special roots called "knees" that stick up out of the water.

PLATE 9

Most bogs are found in cool places. The water in bogs is from precipitation and is too acidic for most types of plants to survive. Some plants that grow in bogs have unusual ways of surviving. Northern Pitcher Plants trap and "eat" insects to get the nutrients they need. Bogs are often covered with a thick carpet of Sphagnum Moss. When the mosses decay, a moist, rich material called "peat" forms. People like to use peat to improve the soil in their gardens.

PLATE 10

Wetland plants provide places for animals to hide from predators. Stems and roots shelter animals both above and below the water. Mangrove swamps are found in salty water along warm or tropical coasts. Red Mangroves have tall roots that stick up above the water and support the tree. They are sometimes called "walking mangroves" because the long roots make the trees look as if they are walking into the water.

PLATE 11

Many different kinds of animals depend on wetlands to provide safe nurseries for their young. Prairie potholes form in holes dug out by the glaciers that covered the land thousands of years ago. The holes fill with water from rain or snow. These marshes are good places for ducks to nest. The prairie pothole region of North America is sometimes called the "duck factory" because so many ducks raise babies there.

PLATE 12

Some animals live in wetlands all the time. Others stay just long enough to find food and water. On their long trips, many migrating animals stop over in wetlands to find food and rest. Animals of all sizes—from large mammals like moose to small birds like tree swallows—depend on wetlands.

PLATE 13

Rice—a wetland plant—provides food for billions of people. Cranberries—bog plants—are one of the few fruits native only to North America that are harvested commercially. Many fish and shellfish go to salt marshes to lay their eggs. After hatching, the babies stay there until they grow large enough to be safe in open water. People all over the world depend on these animals for food.

PLATE 14

The extra water that is stored in wetlands during periods of heavy rain seeps away slowly after the storm. The plants growing in wetlands along rivers slow down floodwaters and help prevent damage. When these riverine wetlands are destroyed, floods cause more destruction. Even the smallest wetlands provide flood protection. Together many small wetlands can hold a large amount of water.

PLATE 15

Estuaries are tidal marshes found where rivers and streams flow into the ocean. The water in tidal marshes rises with high tides and drains with low tides. The plants that grow in estuaries help reduce the power of storm surges. This prevents erosion along the shore and protects the land farther from the coast. Estuaries also help prevent flooding by soaking up extra water during heavy rains.

PLATE 16

Wetlands act as filters that remove pollutants from the water. The roots and stems of wetland plants hold the water long enough for impurities to settle to the bottom. Then when the water seeps back into the ground, the sediment stays behind and the water is cleaned. This helps to keep the water in our wells safe. Wetlands work so well at cleaning water that people often build them to treat wastewater and storm-water runoff.

PLATE 17

Many wetlands have been destroyed because people do not recognize their importance. They are often thought of as useless wastelands that need to be drained or filled. Wetlands of all sizes should be protected in order to keep our world healthy and beautiful.

ABOUT THE SILLS

Cathryn Sill, a former elementary school teacher, is the author of the acclaimed ABOUT… series. With her husband John and her brother-in-law Ben Sill, she coauthored the popular bird-guide parodies, A FIELD GUIDE TO LITTLE-KNOWN AND SELDOM-SEEN BIRDS OF NORTH AMERICA, ANOTHER FIELD GUIDE TO LITTLE-KNOWN AND SELDOM-SEEN BIRDS OF NORTH AMERICA, and BEYOND BIRDWATCHING.

John Sill is a prize-winning and widely published wildlife artist who illustrated the ABOUT… series and coauthored the FIELD GUIDES and BEYOND BIRDWATCHING. A native of North Carolina, he holds a B.S. in Wildlife Biology from North Carolina State University.

The Sills live in Franklin, North Carolina.

Fred Eldredge, Creative Image Photography

Books in the ABOUT… series

ISBN 978-1-56145-028-2 HC
ISBN 978-1-56145-147-0 PB

ISBN 978-1-56145-141-8 HC
ISBN 978-1-56145-174-6 PB

ISBN 978-1-56145-183-8 HC
ISBN 978-1-56145-233-0 PB

ISBN 978-1-56145-207-1 HC
ISBN 978-1-56145-232-3 PB

ISBN 978-1-56145-234-7 HC
ISBN 978-1-56145-312-2 PB

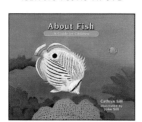

ISBN 978-1-56145-256-9 HC
ISBN 978-1-56145-335-1 PB

ISBN 978-1-56145-038-1 HC
ISBN 978-1-56145-364-1 PB

ISBN 978-1-56145-301-6 HC
ISBN 978-1-56145-405-1 PB

ISBN 978-1-56145-331-3 HC
ISBN 978-1-56145-406-8 PB

ISBN 978-1-56145-358-0 HC